The Golden Book on Writing

The Golden Book on Writing

by David Lambuth

AND OTHERS

Foreword by Budd Schulberg

New York · The Viking Press

Originally published in 1923 by Dartmouth College,
    Hanover, N.H. Republished with new material in 1963
    by S. Heagan Bayles
Reissued with additional new material in 1964 by
The Viking Press, Inc., 625 Madison Avenue,
    New York, N.Y. 10022

Viking Compass edition issued simultaneously

Published simultaneously in Canada by
The Macmillan Company of Canada Limited

Library of Congress catalog card number: 63-13634
Printed in U.S.A. by The Murray Printing Co.

SBN-34396-x (hardbound)
SBN-670-00158-9 (paperbound)

Twelfth printing November 1973

It was an experience, knowing Professor David Lambuth at Dartmouth College thirty years ago. On the outside, Davidlambuth—as his Alice-in-Wonderland wife always called him—was the answer to a freshman's dream of what a college English professor should look like. (This sentence ends with a preposition on good authority —Professor Lambuth's. He was precise but not fussy. He was not a grammarian's grammarian. He was a literary pragmatist. What *worked* was right.) Like his *Golden Book*, Lambuth asked that our writing be clear, vivid, moving. He was a big verb man. He knew the power of our language flowed from verbs that were "busy doing or making something." To think clearly, to think forcefully on paper, he taught us to use active verbs. A classic Lambuthism: Not "When Elizabeth was queen," but "When Elizabeth *reigned*." It is said, with good reason, that no one can teach anyone else how to write. Well, if Lambuth cannot make you drink, at least he turns you in the general direction of the water.

The look of Lambuth, and his eccentricity, hardly prepared you for his uncompromising rejection of pompous sentence structures and prolix paragraphs. He affected pince-nez, a white professorial beard, a rakish black beret, white "Mark Twain" suit and white shoes, a black opera cape, and a white Packard. The white Packard was not an affectation. It was the professor's way of accommodating Mrs. Lambuth's absent-mindedness. It was Mrs. Lambuth's custom to shop along the small Main Street of our college town and drop her purchases in any vehicle that happened to be handy. Professor Lambuth thought a white Packard would stand out among the less spectacular autos parked alongside it. But Mrs. Lambuth had a genius for absent-mindedness. Leaving Tanzi's Grocery Store with an armful of bundles, she deposited them confidently on the front seat of a white milk-wagon. When the driver found them he knew exactly where to deliver them. In fact it became a custom for the milkman to deliver the Lambuth groceries. My first meeting with her still shines in my memory. I had been invited to dinner, and with undergraduate enthusiasm for this rare privilege I was the first guest to arrive. I had visions of sitting near the fire with the learned, pipe-smoking professor to discuss Conrad and Stevenson. Instead an animated lady met me at the door in a long apron over her dinner dress. She handed me a large bowlful of raw string beans. "Since you've come so early, I hope you're good at stringing beans," she said in welcome.

For nearly half an hour I extracted strings from string beans. And this brings me back to this fine little book. For all his flamboyance and theatricality, Professor Lambuth commands our devotion and deserves this republication because he was a bear for pulling the strings—the stringy, unnecessary, indigestible fibers and excesses—from the English sentence, the English paragraph, the sturdy Anglo-Saxon English language. Lambuth was an uncommon man who taught that good writing began with common sense. He was a Flaubertian stickler for the right word. He loved English with a nice passion. Can any other language fuel such a raging bonfire with so few sticks? At its best it provides heat and light, a maximum of thought and emotion, with a minimum of syllables. Shakespeare knew this. Twain and Hemingway. And Frost. Our Davidlambuth was able to put it down in a book short on pages but long on insights. When you write, he said, make a picture with the nouns. And make that picture move with the verbs.

Professor Lambuth rode a white Packard like a white charger into battle against the hordes of bad writing flying the enemy flags of pretension and verbosity. His flag was the deceptively simple *Golden Book on Writing*. Now we pick it up and carry it forward. No extra flourishes, please. No circumlocution curlicues, no rhetorical ringlets. Give it to me straight, says the Lambuth flag. If I may paraphrase another Lambuthism, he had a nail to hit, and in this welcome little bible of a book he practices his preach and hits it on the head.

BUDD SCHULBERG

March 23, 1964

In business, as in many other pursuits, the purpose of writing is to get an idea from one mind into another, clearly, speedily, and economically. The more successfully writing accomplishes this objective, the more it can be considered good writing.

The lack of good writing is perhaps one of the most costly wastes in business. Obviously, foggy writing causes more and more inefficiency as organizations grow bigger and bigger. Bad writing eats up the reading time of highly paid executives, creates misunderstandings and errors, and often makes it necessary to do the job twice at more than twice the cost.

It is in the spirit of developing good writing that we reprint "On Writing" by David Lambuth with a new chapter, "On Business Writing," by Walter O'Meara. Over the years "On Writing" has been especially helpful to me. I hope the knowledge and wisdom encompassed in this new edition proves equally useful to you.

To John Hurd, Professor of English, Dartmouth College, I shall be forever indebted for his encouragement to me as an undergraduate. His colorful foreword to "On Writing" by David Lambuth will give you an insight into the unusual character of the man who wrote the book.

Publisher's Note to the 1963 Edition

S. HEAGAN BAYLES
Chairman of the Board
Sullivan, Stauffer, Colwell & Bayles, Inc.

Bad writing, fatty and foolish, muddy and mucky, sloppy and sleazy. Let's teach them how to write just one good paragraph; indeed, just one good sentence. But how? No effective book on writing exists.

So, in 1923, thought Professor David Lambuth. He is still famous, a picturesque character. Generations of Dartmouth undergraduates gloried in his white suit and black pince-nez ribbon, his black European cape and white beard, his white shoes and black beret.

He drove his white Packard slowly about the elm-lined country streets with the same deliberate old-world charm with which he tossed a green salad or read poetry aloud to students hushed in admiration. He hated slovenly prose. He loved a style based on the good, the beautiful, the true.

Four other men in the Department of English felt almost as passionately about good writing: Kenneth Allan Robinson, Hewette E. Joyce, Benfield Pressey, Anton A. Raven. When Mr. Lambuth proposed collaboration on a book, they said, "Yes—happy to!" They went to work. Their contributions Mr. Lambuth revised, polished, streamlined.

So a book was born. Little it was, tiny, only fifty pages, including a bibliography. Unpretentious, paper-covered, inexpensive. Profits? Who cared? A second edition? Not even considered. Copyright? Yes, we must. But no one ever got around to it.

It was nonetheless a brilliant piece, emerging

from gifted men with a passion for simple, force-ful, controlled, and harmonious prose. Within half a dozen years the edition was exhausted. Later the little book dropped out of sight, but it continued to draw nostalgic sighs from older professors. But try to buy a copy! Try to find one! Impossible. Gone forever.

But not quite.

Now it is rediscovered. Not on the shelf of a Dartmouth professor gone to a Heaven of dis-tinguished prose. Not in a dusty Hanover attic. At, of all places, 575 Lexington Avenue, New York—by the head of an advertising agency as modern as the twenty-first century.

The book and the story are like a hole-in-one in golf. They should send teachers of English who have slogged through the muck and slashed through the fat of college themes back to the educational fairway. What finer tribute than the reprinting of this little book to a man who loved good writing?

PROFESSOR JOHN HURD
Department of English
Dartmouth College

On Writing
by David Lambuth
in collaboration with K. A. Robinson, H. E. Joyce, W. B. Pressey, and A. A. Raven

Contents

[XIV]

On Writing

by David Lambuth

in collaboration with K. A. Robinson,
H. E. Joyce, W. B. Pressey, and A. A. Raven

A Warning

This isn't a textbook of rhetoric. It is the gathering together of some practical suggestions on writing. And as a suggestion on any subject is a good suggestion only in so far as the reason for it is clear, we have tried to give the reason in every case. The advice given is such as some twenty years of experience in editorial office and in personal conference with undergraduates have shown to be most needed and most profitable.

Nobody can lay down rules for anybody else's writing. The particular difficulties which always come up by the score have to be wrestled with as special problems by the man who is trying to capture his own ideas and get them down on paper. There is certainly no advantage in trying to codify all these difficulties—and making fat dull books of them—because, in the first place, they are numberless, and, in the second place, what the 'prentice writer needs to be told is *what to do* and *not what not to do,* and, in the third place, clear thinking and not a mastery of rules and a memory full of difficulties is what makes good writing. Nobody has ever yet learned how to write well by memorizing rules or trying consciously to write by them. Good writing—as I have just remarked—comes only from clear thinking, set down in simple and natural speech, and *afterwards* revised in accordance with good usage. The adequate vocabulary and the feeling for this good usage and idiom which are so essential to good writing can be acquired only by wide and intelligent reading. And in no other way whatsoever.

Use your eyes and ears. Think. Read . . . read . . . and still read. And then, when you have found your idea, don't be afraid of it—or of your pen and paper; write it down as nearly as possible as you would express it in speech; swiftly, un-selfconsciously, without stopping to think about the form of it at all. Revise it afterwards—but only afterwards. To stop to think about form in mid-career, while the idea is in motion, is like throwing out your clutch half-way up a hill and having to start in low again. You never get back your old momentum.

After all, good writing is like good social usage. It is learned by constant association with those who practice it, and it must be instinctive and un-selfconscious before it is of the slightest value. That is why you can learn how to write

well only by reading well. The man who writes
with one eye on the textbook of rhetoric, or one
half of his brain trying to remember rules, is
like the man who can't tell whether to take off
his hat or to use his fork or his spoon until he
has remembered what was said on page 74 or
135 of some so-called "Book of Etiquette." Gentlemen do not act by rules nor learn how to con-
duct themselves out of textbooks. Neither do
good writers.

Therefore: Read . . . read . . . and still read.

The Organization of the Whole

1. Know Where You Are Going

The object of any piece of writing is to make your reader understand exactly what you have to say—and understand it as quickly and as effectively as possible. To make your reader do this you must lay out your article, report, story —whatever it may be—like a carefully surveyed road. Otherwise it will never get anywhere in particular; it will merely stop short after a certain number of pages. For lack of a plan too many pieces of writing find themselves "miserably straggling to an end in sandy deltas." We are all too busy to read that sort of thing.

2. Set Up Sign-Posts

Think of a piece of writing as a trip from a definite starting point to a definite destination. At the very start we look for a sign-post pointing the way and naming the place we are headed

[6]

for. At every fork of the road we need directions —legible and understandable directions. From time to time we glance back over the road we have already come, in order to remind ourselves of our position and direction. At the end we want to know that we have arrived at the point we set out for. Reminders of this sort are just as necessary in writing as they are in posting a road.

Point out to your reader, then, at the beginning, the direction in which you are going and the destination you have in view. Remind him of the progress you are making by setting up easily read sign-posts along the road. At the end tell him clearly that you have arrived—and see that he understands it. Don't have him turning over the page and saying with a start: "Oh, that's all there is to it. . . . Now let's see; where are we?"

The Paragraph

The paragraph is merely a group of more or less closely related sentences which deal with a subdivision of the thought. There is nothing hard and fast about paragraph structure—and never was. The paragraph was developed in order to make reading easier for us by gathering into convenient parcels such statements as go naturally together.

If paragraphs are to assist us in reading, they must do it by having a pretty distinct unity in themselves. Don't make them so long that they are hard to follow, nor so short that they are choppy. Try to make a transition—a bridge-over—either with connective words, or by your handling of the idea itself, from one paragraph to the next so that we shan't feel a bump in crossing over. Take care that the subject of a paragraph is made clear in the paragraph itself and not merely implied from the preceding para-

[8]

graph or referred to by a pronoun. Such a practice, except in rare cases, weakens the unity of the paragraph and leaves the reader in doubt as to just what the subject of it is. Unless a paragraph is more or less self-contained it does not fulfill its mission in life.

There is no absolute rule for paragraphing. Your own feeling must be your guide.

4. Emphasis

The tendency of most of our modern writers is to shorten the paragraph for the sake of greater emphasis. Single sentences are sometimes set off as separate paragraphs. Such paragraphing is sometimes justifiable, but it must be clear that if we attempt to make each sentence emphatic we only make each one equally *un*emphatic. The paragraph is a valuable device. Don't abuse it.

But always remember that the beginning and the end of a paragraph are the most emphatic positions in a piece of writing.

The Sentence

5. What it Is   Now, the sentence was not invented by grammarians—although they sometimes seem to think so—but was developed by ordinary people as the best way of expressing thoughts. The form of the sentence is merely the way in which mankind naturally thinks, the order in which thoughts most easily take shape in our minds. That is why a man who thinks clearly will always find it possible to write a well constructed sentence, and a man who is vague or lazy in his thinking will almost always write a badly constructed sentence. The clearer our thinking, the easier it is to express our thought in its natural form, which, of course, is the form in which it is most easily understood by our readers.

A sentence is merely the setting up of some subject of thought—the *subject*—and the saying of something about it—the *predicate*. It is the

[10]

simplest form in which a complete and independent statement of fact can be made. It is, therefore, the unit of all logical thinking and writing.

A sentence is normally an independent unit, one that stands firmly on its own feet. Hence, if a statement is not complete, if it cannot stand alone and be thoroughly intelligible, we feel that the thought is broken and imperfect. This is the reason why it is objectionable to write subordinate clauses—such as, for example, those beginning with the relatives, *who, which, that,* the conjunction *though,* or the adverb *where*— as though they were complete sentences. *Who left town yesterday. Which he took with him. Though I had seen him before. Where he had been twice.* No one of these four groups of words makes complete sense by itself; therefore they are not sentences. (The use of *who, which, where* interrogatively—*Who left town yesterday?* —is, of course, another matter.)

6. Completeness in the Sentence

Exclamations and phrases such as we constantly hear in everyday speech are not really exceptions to this rule. *Good Heavens! Rather! Just a little.* These are either well-known exclamations which have grown to be good usage or are really sentences with the omitted parts of speech supplied in thought—usually from the preceding sentence. Such elliptical sentences as the last of the three above are not usually written, however, except in quoted speech.

The best modern writing is coming to employ increasingly certain kinds of incomplete sentences and certain groups of words which do not attempt to represent sentences at all. These incomplete sentences are usually of the sort quoted in the second paragraph above: subordinate clauses separated by a period from their principal clauses, as: *I yelled to him to jump. Which he did* . . . This separation—in defiance of older usage—is employed for the sake of emphasis, and is unquestionably allowable if sparingly used by a writer who is mature enough to know just what he is doing. It is a perilous practice, however, for the amateur.

The modern use of groups of words which are without stating verbs and do not even attempt to represent sentences, is an altogether different usage. This innovation in writing, which may be very beautifully used, is an attempt to reflect the impression made upon the mind by some object or event without making any statement concerning it beyond merely registering that impression. As such it is a more adequate representation of some of our simple perceptions—an important part of our mental life—than any other device makes possible. *Clouds, black and boiling. A gust of wind. A white flash from zenith to horizon.* Such phrases paint a picture much more true to the impression made upon the mind of the observer than *The clouds were black and boiling. There was a gust of wind. Then lightning flashed from zenith to horizon.* Fragmentary writing of the kind illustrated above is quite properly called "impressionistic," and is perhaps the most effective development of usage in both modern prose and poetry. But it takes a fine sense of writing and of life to handle it with power. Too frequently used, it loses all its effectiveness and becomes little more than gibberish.

In addition to being complete, a sentence must be unified. We have come to think of a sentence as expressing just one dominant thought, and we are usually misled when it attempts to do more than that. A sentence containing two or more distinctly separate statements lacks unity and ought usually to be broken up into two or more sentences, unless the two statements are so closely related that they depend upon each other for their full meaning.

7. Unity in the Sentence

For the sake of unity it is also much better not to change from one grammatical subject to another in the several parts of a compound sentence and not to introduce too many different subjects in the subordinate clauses of a complex sentence. The more closely the parts and clauses of a sentence can center about[1] one dominating subject, the simpler that subject is for the mind to grasp. Such simplicity is one of the first requirements of careful writing.

Though I had met him before, his face was unfamiliar is a grammatically correct sentence; but *Though I had met him before, I could not remember his face* is simpler and better because it does not change subjects between clauses.

Shifting subjects from clause to clause in a sentence always has the result of decreasing the ease and the speed with which the reader's mind follows the thought.

Your first duty in writing is to make it as easy as possible for your reader to follow your thought. Obscurity is not profundity. Neither is it art.

8. Co-ordination and Subordination of Ideas

A simple sentence is a single statement of fact, or facts, with one subject and one predicate—although this subject may, of course, be made up of more than one item and the predicate of more than one idea. *Dogs are loyal. Both Diehards and Dinmonts have long been noted for their intelligence and prized for their loyalty.*

A compound sentence is a sentence made up of two or more independent statements joined together. *All dogs are loyal, and Diehards are the most loyal of all.*

A complex sentence is a sentence made up of two or more distinct statements, of which only one is independent, the others being dependent upon the main statement for their full meaning. *Although all dogs are loyal, the Irish terrier is the most loyal. The Irish terrier, which may be either wire-haired or curly, is an unusually clever dog.*

Simple sentences are naturally the clearest and the most direct, but employed exclusively they are disjointed, monotonous, and almost childish. They no more build up thought than isolated bricks build a house, because every statement stands alone and has equal weight with every other statement.

Compound sentences make possible a rudimentary grouping of statements, and by so much help to build up organized thinking. But they do not make it possible to distinguish clearly between the importance of the several connected statements, and the sentence becomes stringy. Compound sentences are like bricks laid end to end, but not articulated in a coherent bond.

Complex sentences alone make possible that careful indication of the importance of one idea over another and that sense of the interrelation of ideas which is essential to accurate thinking. Not until you have learned to select almost unconsciously the central, dominating thought of your sentence, and to group around this in varying degrees of emphasis the secondary or modifying thoughts, have you learned to think clearly.

In the revision of your work take pains to distinguish between ideas and statements which are co-ordinate, that is, of equal importance to the progress of the thought, and those which are subordinate to the main thought, that is, are of importance only as they help to make this main thought clearer. It would be only pedantry to list here the varieties of subordinate clauses and their shifting shades of meaning. The proper handling of clauses doesn't depend on a knowledge of their names. It depends upon a piece of thinking which has been careful and clear enough to grasp the logical relationship of the ideas you are putting into words.

Johnson's opportunities had been limited; he studied his job and made a success. The several statements made here seem to be intelligible enough, it is true; but because the sentence doesn't emphasize the most important idea and subordinate the others, it fails to say exactly what the writer had in mind. The important idea is undoubtedly the fact that Johnson succeeded, *in spite* of lack of opportunities, *because* of hard study. Proper subordination will not only state all the original ideas but also bring out their exact relationship. *Although Johnson's opportunities had been limited, he made a success because he studied his job.*

Your thinking is not done, nor your writing either, when you have merely stated your several ideas. Your thinking is not done until you have fully and clearly indicated the interrelation between these ideas. Sills, joists, studs, and rafters do not make a house until they have been assembled into a carefully planned and carefully fitted structure. All this seems trite and obvious, of course, and yet three-fourths—if not nine-tenths—of the bad writing in the world is bad because it fails to put its sentence elements logically together.

9. The Frontal Attack A sentence is only a sort of moving picture of thought, and the picture will have the clearest continuity when it follows most closely the natural order of our thinking. This means that the thing thought about—the *subject*—should usually appear near the beginning of the sentence; and that what is thought about it—the *predicate*—should follow after, with the various modifying elements—clauses, phrases, and so on—introduced in the order in which they naturally come to the mind in its onward movement. This natural sentence order may be varied for many good reasons; but, in general, if you will keep your subject close to the beginning of your sentence, you will find both your thinking and your sentence the clearer for it.

● When a sentence doesn't seem to be going well it is a good thing to stop and ask yourself "What is it I am really talking about in this sentence?" When you have discovered exactly what this central idea is and have put it down as the subject of the sentence you will usually find that the thought unrolls itself far more easily—and far more intelligibly for the reader.

More of a dealer's goods may be sold by a simple and convincing advertisement than by a freakish one is, of course, grammatically correct, but if what we are really talking about is the *quality of a good advertisement,* instead of a *quantity of dealer's goods,* we should find it both simpler and clearer to write: *A simple and convincing advertisement sells more goods than a freakish one.*

If you have a nail to hit, hit it on the head.

Writing sentences which are easily understood frequently depends upon keeping sentence ele-

10. The Natural Order

ments in their natural or logical order. Many sentences are ineffective because their various elements seem to have been flung together haphazard. This confusion can generally be avoided by a little careful thinking. Remember that the three simplest kinds of order—the order of time, the order of cause to effect, and the order of climax—are particularly useful in helping you to arrange details in a natural and easy series. *He flung himself over the cliff, crazed with jealousy* reverses the order in time, puts effect before cause, and is an anti-climax. The sentence would carry its meaning more clearly and more forcefully if reversed: *Crazed with jealousy, he flung himself over the cliff.*

We must not forget, however, that an unnatural order may be justified if it serves the purpose of emphasis and is judiciously handled. When the reason for an act is introduced by *for* at the end of a sentence, it is weak because it is evidently added as an afterthought and reverses the order of time and of cause to effect. On the other hand, *because,* which is a much more emphatic word, may very well introduce a clause which has been held over to the end of the sentence for emphasis. Note the lack of emphasis in *I came to dinner for I was hungry* as compared with *I came to dinner because I was hungry.* Notice, however, the difference in the effect secured by using the logical order: *Because I was hungry, I came to dinner.*

Always be careful not to separate a subject too far from its verb by piling up modifying elements between the two. Subjects and verb are closely bound in thought; too great separation tends to break the connection and obscure the meaning.

Be even more particular to keep the verb as close to its object as possible. The active force in a verb should pass readily over to its object; obstacles between the two slow down the flow of thought.

It is usually desirable to keep the parts of a compound verb together. *I have seen him there whenever I visited the house* is better than *I have, whenever I visited the house, seen him there.*

⁜ A sentence is intended to carry the mind on from the subject to the predicate in the simplest way. This carrying on—this transference of thought—is the work of the verb; to do it well the verb needs to be prominent and active. But the necessary prominence and activity of the main verb is often lost behind what is called "excessive predication." Excessive predication is a result of the lazy habit of using more verbs than are necessary—of winding up, as it were, before coming to your point.

The habit of beginning statements with the impersonal and usually vague *there is* or *there are* shoves the really significant verb into subordinate place instead of letting it stand vigorously on its own feet. In place of saying *A brick house stands on the corner,* you find yourself

11. The Vice of Excessive Predication

lazily falling into *There is a brick house which stands on the corner.* In the latter sentence the attention is first directed to *there is,* and from that to *stands,* which ought to have had the whole emphasis, because it is the one definite statement in the sentence.

We walked down the main street, which was very long distracts the attention by making two statements where only one was needed. *We walked down the long main street* is a simpler and for that reason a more effective statement. At first sight it may seem that the clause *which was very long* draws the reader's attention to the length of the street more emphatically than the single adjective *long.* But the contrary is true. In the first place, the fewer the words that can be made to convey an idea, the clearer and the more forceful that idea. In the second place, the more ideas the writer can suggest to the reader by single words and phrases rather than by complete statements in clauses—such as, *long main street* instead of *main street which was very long*—the more vividly the reader's imagination catches up the ideas and realizes them. Offering the reader the material and leaving him to work this material up into complete statements, if he wishes to do so, engages his imagination more effectively than working the whole thing out for him. Modern "impressionism" in writing is a recognition of this fact.

Remember, furthermore, that each sentence ought to concentrate on some dominant relationship between ideas—the relationship that is

usually expressed in the stating verb. The more
statements you make in a sentence, the less
vividly the principal statement stands out. In
other words, concentrate on your central idea.
Complexities frequently have to be introduced
because the meaning demands it, but don't introduce complexities and scatter your reader's attention merely because you are too careless to
pick out and emphasize the significant point.

Words, phrases and even clauses are often introduced into a sentence to modify, that is, to limit
or to tell something more about particular words
or statements. These modifiers must be placed so
that they modify the right words and no others.

I decided when I had finished the job to quit
leaves us uncertain whether *when I had finished
the job* is meant to modify *decided* or *to quit*.
When I had finished the job I decided to quit
or *I decided to quit when I had finished the job*
resolves the confusion by placing the modifying
clause in an unambiguous position.

It is a mishandling of modifiers that works
havoc in the "dangling participle." Except where
the participle is used as a noun—Latinistic grammarians call it the "gerund"—as in "Parting is
such sweet sorrow," it is an adjective form and
must modify some definite noun or pronoun in
the clause. If this noun or pronoun is missing,
the participle attaches itself to some other noun,
and confusion results. *Crossing the campus College Hall disclosed itself* makes nonsense because

**12. Modifiers
and Where
to Put Them**

we, the pronoun which *crossing* should modify, does not appear in the sentence. *As we were crossing the campus, etc.,* would avoid the difficulty. Such errors are always the result of careless writing.

It is always essential to read over carefully what you have written, in order to see whether the meaning has anywhere been obscured by an ambiguous placing of modifying elements. And this re-reading should be done some time after the writing has been finished. You understand just what you mean so clearly at the moment when you are doing the writing that it is exceedingly hard for you to recognize ambiguities. Not even the best writer can weigh judicially a page that is hot from the pen—or the typewriter. After the writing is "cold" the ambiguities stare you in the face—at least they ought to. Later revision of this kind is much better than writing with painful slowness in the first draft. Snail-pace writing never catches up with spontaneity—which is one of the greatest of the literary virtues.

13. Making Reference Unmistakable

The personal pronouns: *he, him, she, her, it, they,* and *them,* the relative pronouns: *who, whom, which,* and *that,* and the demonstrative pronouns: *this, that, these,* and *those,* often refer back to some preceding noun or substantive phrase, grammatically called the antecedent. The sense of a sentence often depends upon this reference being[2] exact and clear. Since pro-

nouns have an awkward habit of attaching themselves to whatever substantive happens to be
nearest them, they must be handled with care.

1. Obviously a pronoun must agree in person,
gender, and number with its antecedent. If there
are two or more antecedents, the relative* must,
of course, be plural, even though each of the
antecedents is a singular.

2. A relative pronoun should always be placed
as near as possible to its antecedent, and no
other substantive to which the relative might
grammatically refer should be allowed to slip in
between the relative and its proper antecedent.
I found my tie in the drawer which I had lost
fails to say what the writer intended because the
relative *which* is carelessly placed after *drawer*
and therefore refers to it, whereas it was meant
to refer to *tie*.

3. A personal or possessive pronoun is ordinarily used to refer to the subject of the sentence or to an emphatic word in the sentence.
Hence it is better not to confuse the reader—
even for a moment—by allowing the pronoun to
refer to some other word, even though the grammatical agreement with such word is correct.
*Just as Smith stopped to speak to Jones a car ran
over him* is, of course, grammatically correct if

---

* "Relative" appears to be a slip of the pen for "pronoun." This rule applies to all kinds of pronouns. There
is, however, a common exception: the case of two
or more antecedents expressing the same idea—in which
case, of course, the pronoun will be singular. *He had the
will, the desire, the determination, and this kept him
going.*—ED.

him refers to *Jones.* But it is momentarily confusing, nevertheless. The reader is thinking in terms of *Smith* and, at first reading, instinctively takes *him* to refer to *Smith.* Such uncertainties should be avoided.

4. A pronoun should not ordinarily refer to a noun in the possessive case. *This hat is my friend's who just left* is excessively awkward.

5. A pronoun should not ordinarily be made to refer to a noun which is implied but not expressed. *He succeeded, which he attributed to hard work* is loose writing. Nevertheless, such reference may be justified when, for instance, the attempt to avoid it results in such ungainly stiffness as: *He succeeded, which fact he attributed to hard work.*

14. Keeping Parallelism Parallel

We often find it necessary to compare or contrast ideas in parallel or balanced phrases, clauses, or sentences. Most of our thinking, in fact, consists in setting off one idea against another. It is easy to see that where two ideas or groups of ideas are to be contrasted or set side by side in this way, they should be worded in similar form so as to make the contrast or parallelism obvious at once to the eye.

The sentence *He was a good reader but I did not care much for what he wrote* throws the mind off the track by failing to state parallel ideas in a strictly parallel form. *He was a good reader but a poor writer* emphasizes the parallelism and brings out the meaning. A salesman who is trying to prove the superiority of his lubricating oil does not compare the effect of his oil in a motor gear-case with the effect of his rival's oil on a squeaky hinge. He compares the two oils in the gear-case of the same car.

Statements which are almost, but not quite, parallel are always confusing. The statement *Thompson made a million, but Taylor made a failure in business* perplexes us because it takes an unexpected turn. The idea could be more effectively expressed by *Thompson made a million, but Taylor lost every cent he had,* or *Thompson made a success, but Taylor made a failure.*

If articles, prepositions, or conjunctions appear before one word in a series of parallel words, they should usually be repeated before the other words as well. Furthermore, when such pairs as *either . . . or, neither . . . nor, whether . . . or; both . . . and,* or *not only . . . but also,* are used before parallel words, phrases or clauses, the words, phrases, or clauses which follow one member of the pair should be as nearly as possible in the same form—as to modifiers, articles, and so on—as those which follow the other member of the pair. *He wore both hat and coat* or *He wore both a hat and a coat;* not *He wore both a hat and coat. He neither ate nor drank;* not *He neither ate nor did he drink.*

If you can do so without making the effect monotonous, it is well to apply the principle of parallelism to sentences and even to large units whenever the meaning lends itself to such treatment.

15. Playing Up Emphasis

There are two emphatic positions in a sentence, a paragraph, or a larger whole. These are the beginning and the end. The beginning is emphatic because it catches the reader's attention first, but the end is emphatic because it makes the last impression. What we hear last is usually the most vivid to us.

Unless you have good reason for doing otherwise, put your most important word or phrase at the end of the sentence. The most important word is usually a substantive or a verb. Don't sacrifice the strategic final position to a preposition or even to an adverb, unless it really is the most significant word—which it sometimes is. The well-known advice against ending a sentence with a preposition is valid only against unimportant prepositions. In certain cases a preposition is the most emphatic word to end a sentence with.

In a group of statements such as make up a paragraph, each succeeding statement tends to push the preceding from the mind and to become in its turn the center of attention. The last sentence should, therefore, usually be the focus or conclusion of the paragraph. And in a properly constructed essay, article, or report the last paragraph should usually state the conclusion the reader is intended to carry away.

Build *up to* your big idea, not *down from* it.

NOTE: This Section 15 illustrates in sentence formation, in paragraph structure, and in the organization of the whole section, the statements made concerning the placing of emphasis.

Words

Good writing, whether in an article, a story, or a business statement, must be clear, accurate, and vivid. Whether you are clear or not depends to a considerable degree upon the clearness of your sentence structure, but your accuracy and vividness depend upon the words you use.

Your words must fit the exact shade of your meaning. Ill-chosen words, words that are vague or misleading, give away the fact that you have been too lazy to think clearly what you are trying to say or else that you don't quite know what words mean. The only satisfactory way to enlarge a poverty-stricken vocabulary is to read widely. You really come to know words and their shades of meaning only by meeting and getting acquainted with them in their proper context, for the sense for words is an instinctive feeling rather than any self-conscious and laborious attainment.

16. Exact Words for Exact Thoughts

There is rarely more than one right word to express an idea exactly. See that you get that one right word.

According to Gustave Flaubert, one of the great masters of realism, success in expression depends upon getting the one right word and conveying by it that individual quality of a thing which distinguishes it from all others. He said to his friend and disciple Guy de Maupassant: "Whatever the thing you wish to say, there is but one word to express it, but one verb to give it movement, but one adjective to qualify it; you must seek until you find this noun, this verb, this adjective. . . . When you pass a grocer sitting in his doorway, a porter smoking a pipe, or a cab stand, show me that grocer and that porter . . . in such a way that I could never mistake them for any other grocer or porter; and by a single word give me to understand wherein one cab horse differs from fifty others before or behind it." Perhaps Flaubert exaggerated a little for emphasis, but the principle is sound. This word game is a fascinating game—and worth the trying.

17. Strong and Active Words at Work

Nouns and verbs are the bones and sinews of speech. Nouns build up the bony structure of the sentence, verbs produce motion. The more concrete nouns and active verbs you use, the more forceful your writing. The novice naturally imagines that piling up adjectives adds definiteness and that sticking in adverbs adds intensity, but it is usually just the other way round. Adjectives and adverbs are often necessary to complete your meaning and make it exact, but they lessen the force of the sentence unless you dole them out stingily as a miser doles out gold. When you divide your reader's attention between a noun and its qualifying adjectives, or between a verb and its adverbs, you decrease the force of the impression which that noun and that verb would normally make. The fewer the words used, the more concentrated the attention; and the greater the concentration, the greater the power. For this reason two or three adjectives pyramided upon each other's shoulders decrease the force of the impression instead of adding to it. At first sight this may not seem reasonable, but it is true.

"The adjective," said Voltaire, "is the enemy of the noun."

Reduce your adjectives and adverbs to a minimum by choosing your nouns and verbs so carefully that they don't need outside assistance in order to convey your meaning. In emotional prose a larger number of adjectives may be needed to supply color, but it is well to remember that even here adjectives thrown into the predicate—that is, attached to the subject by a verb—make a sharper impression than those that immediately qualify a noun.

The clouds rose black, threatening carries more force than *Black, threatening clouds rose.*

And outside—night! is a more vivid and forceful suggestion to the imagination of your reader than *And outside—black, lowering, mysterious night!* You may not believe that at first—but think it over. The psychological law involved is this: the more you can leave to your reader's own imagination to conjure up for itself, the more vivid the picture it builds, provided only, of course, that you have given enough of an initial shove to set his imagination to work.

Verbs are the sinews of speech. They have tremendous potential power.

As far as possible choose verbs which picture or imply action. The most effective verbs are those which are busy doing or making something, rather than those which passively indicate relationship. *"Through the maze of streets Fifth Avenue marches like a central theme."*

Use your verbs in the active voice rather than in the quiescent passive, except, of course, where you want to suggest passivity. *He achieved the presidency* suggests the activity of the candidate more effectively than *He was made president.*

The church stood upon the hilltop makes us see the picture more vividly than *The church had been raised upon the hilltop.*

Remember, finally, that the handy verb *to be* is the weakest of all verbs because it says nothing of itself—it merely joins two ideas together with a colorless glue. *When Elizabeth reigned* says much more of that lady than *When Elizabeth was queen.*

You can always improve a piece of writing by going over it and substituting, as far as possible, active verbs for passive, and specific, motion-depicting verbs for such colorless verbs as *to be, have, seem,* and the rest of that overworked family.

Specific words are always more vivid than general words. Specific words paint pictures of particular, individual objects; general words lump these individual objects together more or less vaguely into a class. The difference between the two is the difference between the photograph of some particular pretty girl and the composite photograph of a thousand pretty girls. One is clear-cut, the other is hazy.

General terms are necessary to scientific statement. Gathering objects or impressions together into classes, drawing inferences from particulars to the general, is an intellectual process which sets man's mind above that of the animal, but such generalized terms should be used only where they are essential to the thought. Their constant and unnecessary intrusion into your writing means that you have failed to observe carefully or to think clearly or to express yourself accurately. Usually it just means that you have been lazy.

General phrasing: *A man was talking to the laborers.*

Specific phrasing: *Revensky, the communist, was haranguing the ditch-diggers.*

Concrete words are more vivid than abstract words. Concrete words are those which stand for material things which may be seen, touched,

tasted, smelled, or heard. Abstract words stand
for ideas conceived by the mind alone, abstract
qualities and conceptions which have been built
up in the mind and have no objective or out-
ward reality. (The vagueness of this attempt at
explaining the word *abstract* is in itself an illustration of the quality of abstractness.)

Your physical experiences, the things you have
seen and heard and touched, are much more
vivid to you than the abstractions of the mind.
To talk in concrete words is to talk in pictures.
The names of concrete objects, sounds, move-
ments set your memory and imagination actively
at work and you see and hear and feel over
again with much of the vividness which these
experiences have had for you in your actual life.
For this reason concrete words are always more
clear-cut, more interesting, and more moving
than abstract ones. *The arch of elms over Main
Street* and *Dartmouth Hall* are concrete, and
vividly present to our senses even when repre-
sented only by words; but *symmetrical beauty
in nature* and *graceful symmetry in architecture,*
which convey the same ideas in abstract form,
fade away into mistiness.

Writing too largely in abstract terms is one of
the worst and most wide-spread of literary
faults. It sounds learned; it saves the writer from
having to use his eyes and ears; and it makes
slovenly thinking possible because it does not
require definiteness. For all these reasons it
damns itself. Inasmuch as man is a rationalizing
animal abstract terms are necessary, but the ordinary writer should make it an inflexible rule

never to use an abstract term if a concrete one will serve. Appeal directly to your reader's emotions rather than indirectly through the intermediary of an intellectualizing process. Tell him that the man *gave a dollar to the tramp* rather than that he *indulged in an act of generosity.*

Abstract: *He gave vehement and conclusive expression to his anger.*

Concrete: *His fist landed squarely on the man's chin and put him down and out.*

Abstract: *Mortal existence is characterized by its transitoriness and its fallacious appearance of importance.*

Concrete: *All the world's a stage, and all the men and women merely players.*

20. Simple Words for Big Ideas

Don't try to seem learned or literary or profound by using long or unfamiliar words. Although there is much mistaken opinion to the contrary, literary English does not demand a stiff, stilted Latinistic vocabulary. It demands the simplest words, the most familiar words, the most concrete words consistent with accurate expression and good every-day usage. As far as possible a writer should write in the very words in which he does his thinking. These are usually simple, homely words. To translate such words into what is too often considered "literary" language results in sacrificing directness, lessening individuality—the greatest of all literary virtues—smudging out the color, and often obscuring even the sense.

This warning against "literary" language is not

intended as an excuse for slovenly writing. Slovenly writing comes from slovenly thinking, and both are anathema. But when you have thought carefully through what you want to say you will find that you can always express yourself more naturally, and therefore more effectively, by using, as far as possible, the familiar words in which your thought shapes itself in your mind.

The homely, concrete, Anglo-Saxon words in which we naturally think and speak are more effective in writing than the more abstract Latinisms. The over-abundant use of Latinisms in our literature is an unhappy heritage from the days when literature was an imitation of Latin and French models instead of a native English product. That part of our vocabulary which has come to us through the French from the Latin has added greatly to the reach and exactness of the English language, but it is valuable as an addition to our stock of Anglo-Saxon words, not as a substitute for it. The objection that Latin derivatives are better fitted than Anglo-Saxon to express profound or exalted emotions is sufficiently disproved by pointing out that the King James Version of the English Bible has the largest proportion of Anglo-Saxon words of any book in our literature. Yet the Bible speaks with an emotional power and with a majesty and music no other book can equal. The Bible deals with the most intense and universal of human emotions: it speaks directly to the heart; it does not concern itself with scientific technicalities or philosophical subtleties. Our Latin derivatives may often clothe the literature of thought; our Anglo-Saxon words give us the literature of power.

The best rule for writing—as well as for speaking—is to use always the simplest words that will accurately convey your thought.

Do not confuse the reader by using different words—or clumsy circumlocutions—to refer to the same object or idea. Repeat the word first used. Such repetitions, instead of being a fault, are often essential to clarity.

21. Elegant Variation and Inelegant Results

The familiar warning against repetition is intended solely to prevent the lazy use of the same word in a variety of different meanings. The constant repetition of such words as *thing, time, good, fine* and many others, with an almost infinite number of meanings, is a case in point. *It is always a good thing to buy a thing that is good* is bad writing, not because *thing* and *good* are repeated, but because they are repeated with different meanings. The result is vagueness. *It is wise to buy only the best* saves space and increases accuracy.

Intelligent repetition is one of the most effective means of securing emphasis. *The sky was gray, the leaves were gray—life itself was gray.*

The would-be elegant sentence: *He saw the white blanket of winter on the road, he felt the powdery crystals upon his face, he tasted the flaky coldness, he seemed even to smell snow,* would be much more vivid writing if simplified thus: *He saw snow on the road, he felt snow on his face, he tasted snow, he seemed even to smell snow.*

22. Euphony and Rhythm

Avoid combinations of words which, because of clashing consonants, are difficult to pronounce. Even though the reader does not read aloud, such harshness makes the words difficult to follow and thus breaks the movement of the thought. *The ugly cacophony of harsh and sibilant syllables* is a sufficient illustration.

Much hasty writing of today is full of tongue-twisters and of broken and jerky rhythm. In this matter no satisfactory rules can be given. The only way to avoid such faults is to train the ear by much reading of good literature and by constantly reading one's own writing aloud. If you find it hard to read your sentences aloud, you may be quite sure your reader will find them unpleasant to read even to himself.

Every mechanical flaw in the writing lessens the ease with which the reader follows the ideas expressed, and to just that degree lessens the effectiveness of the writing.

23. Commonly Misused Words and Phrases

Anywhere, not *anywheres* or *anyplace.*
Behind or *back of,* not *in back of.*
Different from or *different to,*[3] not *different than.*
That kind of flower or *those kinds of flowers* rather than *those kind of flowers.*

Little if any or *rarely if ever*, not *little of any* or *rarely or ever*.

In hope of, not *in hopes of*.

Try to come, rather than *try and come*

A long way, not *a long ways*.

He stayed at home, not *he stayed home*. The best usage omits only the preposition *to* before *home* in cases where *home* is the object of a verb of motion. *He came home*.

Got, rather than *gotten*.

Distinguish between *most* and *almost*. *Almost anybody*, not *most anybody*. *It is almost noon*. not *It is most noon*. *Most*, except when used to form the superlative of adjectives, is a noun used in the sense of *a majority, a large part*. *Almost* is an adverb and means *nearly*.

Distinguish between *owing* and *due*. *Owing to* means *because of, on account of; due to* means *the result of*. For example: *Owing to bad weather the race was delayed. The winning of the race was due to good seamanship*. *Owing* may be used at the beginning of a sentence in the sense of *because of; due* should not be so used.

The more technical statement of this distinction is that the participle *owing* has come to be used as part of a prepositional phrase and does not have to be attached directly to a noun, as in the example cited. *Due*, on the other hand, is an adjective and must directly modify a noun, as in the second example. You cannot say *Due to the rain the game was delayed*, because *game* is evidently the only noun which *due* can modify, and the *game* was evidently not *due to* the *rain.*

Careless newspaper usage is obliterating this distinction, but it is still good English.

Distinguish between *its,* the possessive pronoun, and *it's,* the contraction for *it is. It's time to regrind its valves.*

Distinguish between the intransitive *lie* and the transitive *lay.*

Lie, lay, lain; but *lay, laid, laid.*

Present: *I lie down,* but *I lay the book down.*

Past: *I lay down,* but *I laid the book down.*

Past-Perfect: *I had lain down,* but *I had laid the book down.*

Do as I do, not *Do like I do.*

It looks like rain or *It looks as if it would rain,* not *It looks like it would rain.*

A sort (kind) of game, not *A sort (kind) of a game.*

I was somewhat disappointed, not *I was kind of disappointed.*

I could not help going or *I could but go,* rather than the clumsy *I could not help but go,* which is a contraction of the tautological *I could not help doing anything but go.*

Either, neither, none, anyone are singulars and require the singular verb. There are cases, however, when *none* is used so evidently in a collective sense that the plural verb is justified because a singular would seem stilted.

Usage demands that *too* shall not be the first word in a clause or sentence when it is used as a conjunction meaning *likewise, also, moreover,* or *besides.* In these cases *too* must follow the word or phrase to which it refers. *So, too, I found. He too discovered it. Too* precedes the word it modifies only when it is used as an adverb in the sense of *more than enough, an excessive quantity,* etc. *Too much haste makes waste.*

The grammatical connectives *and, but, or,* etc., regularly precede the words they introduce; but the logical connectives, such as *however, moreover, nevertheless, on the other hand,* usually do their work more successfully when embedded in the group of words to which they are attached.

Only must immediately precede the word or phrase which it modifies. *He only intimated that he asked a dollar, He intimated that he only asked a dollar,* and *He intimated that he asked only a dollar* all mean different things.

Avoid "splitting the infinitive" by inserting an adverb between *to* and its verb. *He ought surely to come,* not *He ought to surely come.* There is occasional justification for "splitting the infinitive," but it is much safer to avoid it altogether.

While means *during the time that,* and is not a synonym for *but. I waited while he went home* and *I waited but he went home* mean two different things.

Don't be misled into using the absurd piece of would-be pedantry *Somebody's else hat,* which is neither good grammar nor good English idiom. *Somebody else's hat* is the only possible usage. *Else* comes from the Anglo-Saxon adjective meaning *other,* and *somebody else* means simply some *other person. Somebody else,* like all other such compounds in English, takes the possessive *s* at the end of the phrase, as for example: *The King of England's crown.* *Somebody's else hat* means *somebody's other hat*— which is not at all what you intend to say.

Avoid the loose use of such overworked words and phrases as: *proposition, along this line, viewpoint, in regard to, quite a little, witness, transpire.* Incidentally, *to transpire* means *to come to light;* it does not mean *to happen.*

Don't use *and* before *which,* except where the *and* is needed to connect two *which* clauses. *Which,* because of its relative function, is itself already a connective, and practically means "*and it*" or "*and they.*" Hence we cannot say *He shows a brilliant style and which distinguishes all his work;* we say *He shows a brilliant style which distinguishes all his work.* Where, however, we want to show that two *which's* introduce co-ordinate clauses we have to use *and* before the second *which,* as: *He shows a brilliant style, which was carefully acquired, and which distinguishes all his work.*

Avoid slang. It is sometimes picturesque and vivid, but it is used lazily to cover such a multitude of meanings that it has lost all accuracy. It may lend color, but it blurs definition. When you do use slang, don't put it in quotation marks. Have the courage of your convictions and write it as an integral part of your sentence.

24. Shall or Will   Grammarians have made the rule for the use of *shall* and *will* unnecessarily confusing because they have tried to approach the problem from the standpoints both of the person speaking and of the grammatical subject of the verb. The difficulty can be avoided. *Will* is derived from the Anglo-Saxon *willan,* which means *to will, to wish, to be about to. Shall* is from the Anglo-Saxon *sculan,* which means *ought, to owe, to be obliged.* The Anglo-Saxon had no future tense. It used the present instead. Gradually *shall* and *will* came to be combined with other verbs to make a compounded future form. They still retain very largely their old meanings.

The distinction between *will* and *shall* is fundamentally the distinction between active and passive; between acting and being acted upon; between being definitely responsible for an action, and being the inactive object or recipient of it. *Will* implies that the force which produces an action comes from inside the person or thing to which *will* refers. *Shall* implies that this force comes from outside the person or thing to which *shall* refers. In order to simplify the discussion as far as possible we will distinguish between the use of *will* and *shall* as it concerns persons and as it concerns things, although the principle is the same for both.

I. The general rule may be stated as follows:

Use *will* when the person referred to is to act of his own free will or purpose; in other words, when he acts as a result of conscious intention. Use *shall* when the person referred to is forced or obliged to act by some influence outside of his own will, or when the action takes place without any conscious intention or determination on the part of the person performing it.

This rule holds equally whether *will* and *shall* refer to the first person or to the second and third persons.

I will leave tomorrow means that I have definitely made up my mind on the subject and that I propose to act in accordance with the dictates of my own will. *I shall leave tomorrow* means either that I am being forced by circumstances that I cannot control, by duty, or by other persons, or merely that I am announcing a future event which I can foresee but with which my will has not been in any way concerned.

He will leave tomorrow means that he will leave of his own free will. (Force from inside.) *He shall leave tomorrow* means that he is being compelled by some force outside himself to leave. (This force may be exerted by me, or by someone else, or even by some series of events over which "he" has no control.)

These examples should make it clear that in general our usage conforms to the original meaning and history of *will* and *shall*. Unfortunately, however, there is a practical complication which seems, at first sight, to violate the rule just given. As an actual fact it doesn't, but the complication needs to be explained. The complication has two phases.

(A) When we use the first person—"I" or "we" —we have the most accurate, "inside" information, and can tell unhesitatingly whether free will or determination is or is not involved. But

when we use the second or third persons—"you,"
"he," "she," "they"—the issue is not so simple.
We cannot know accurately the mental processes
of any person other than ourselves, so that we
find it hard sometimes to tell whether this other
person is acting of his own free will or not. In
order to be on the safe side, therefore, we have
fallen into the habit of politely crediting the
other person with free will, *unless* we know definitely that some sort of force is being exerted
upon him from without. Hence we use *will* in
many doubtful cases in the second and third
persons where we should be more likely to use
shall if we were speaking for the first person. In
other words: we use *shall* for the second and
third persons *only where we know definitely* that
the will of the person referred to is not in any
way involved. In all other cases we feel that it
is safer to use *will*.

(B) It follows from what has just been said
that when we do fetch up our courage and say
He shall go today or *They shall go tomorrow* it
is because we know definitely of some outside
force that will bring the event about. This bold
admission of knowledge on our part makes it
look as though we must be "on the inside," that
is, that we have had a hand in the force or compulsion ourselves. Hence it has come about that
the use of *shall* for the second and third persons
usually suggests force or determination on the
part of the speaker. This inference may, of
course, be true—it often is—but it is by no means
necessarily so. The best English usage by no

means always implies it. For example: *You shall get your book tomorrow* does not necessarily mean that I am forcing you to get the book or that I am going to see to it myself that you do get it; it means merely that the book will come to you without volition or action on your part.

Seek and ye shall find; knock and it shall be opened unto you.

The result of these two complications is that in actual practice we pretty consistently use *shall* with any of the persons—first, second, or third—*only* when we know definitely that some sort of outside pressure, or some sort of circumstances not involving volition, is responsible for the action; in practically all other cases we play safe and use *will*.

II. The rule given for *will* and *shall* applies to inanimate objects and events as well as to persons. But inanimate objects and events can evidently have no conscious will of their own. Therefore, when we use *will* we imply that the thing or event spoken of acts or takes place through some inherent force, quality, or nature of its own; and when we use *shall* we imply that some outside force is working on it. Thus we say *The sun will rise tomorrow* because rising is a part of the nature of the sun; and we say *The book will fall* because falling is an inevitable physical result of the position the book is occupying. If we said *The Sun shall not rise tomorrow* we should mean that some outside force is going to prevent it.

The sun shall not set ere I have my revenge is the statement of a situation with which the nature or movement of the sun has nothing to do; hence the use of *shall.* It should be noted here, by the way, that the speaker is not in the least implying that he is going to use any force upon the sun; the sun appears in the matter only incidentally, as a sort of timepiece.

III. *Should* and *would* follow the rule laid down for *shall* and *will. Should* has retained in a very vigorous fashion the old Anglo-Saxon sense of obligation imposed from without, so that in many cases it has almost the sense of *ought* or *must*; but this meaning must not be allowed to obscure its other meaning of a mere absence of will or purpose—a future act or event in which the will is not involved. *He said that he would go* indicates conscious purpose. *He said that he should go* might mean either that he felt that he ought to go, or that he recognized the fact that he was going, without having made the act of going the result of deliberate intention.

Henry James writes in one of his letters: "*I should be delighted to see you, but I would not advise you to come.*" He used *would* because he thought of his definite intention not to advise his friend's coming. He used *should* because the act of being delighted was not one which made any demand on his will power—it was a matter of course, outside of volition.

In actual practice the meanings of *will, shall, would,* and *should* shade so gradually into each other and depend so largely upon the intent of the writer that it is often difficult for anyone else to judge the accuracy of the usage. This does

not, however, justify a careless use of a beautifully subtle distinction.

NOTE. For the benefit of those who prefer the
old rule invented by seventeenth-century grammarians to account for a usage they did not
wholly understand, we give it in brief, with its
amusing inconsistencies.

(1) Use *shall* for the first person to denote
future action; use *will* for the second and third
persons. (2) Use *will* for the first person to denote promise or determination; use *shall* for the
second and third persons to denote compulsion
by the speaker. (3) Use *shall* in the second and
third persons to convey promises, threats, and
commands. Inasmuch as Rules 1, 2, and 3 are
not infrequently inconsistent with actual practice: (4) In the case of questions and answers
the questioner must first anticipate whether the
person questioned will use *shall* or *will* in his
answer and must then frame his question so that
the same form is used—even though this violates
the usage laid down in Rule 1. (5) In the case of
indirect discourse, although *would* and *should*
ordinarily follow the use of *will* and *shall,* when
we change such a sentence as *"I shall come tomorrow"* into indirect discourse, it is necessary
to substitute *would* for *shall* and say *"He said
that he would come tomorrow."* (6) In the case
of a sentence expressing contingency, use *should*
for all three persons in the conditional clause
(protasis); and ordinarily use *would* for all three
persons in the conclusion (apodasis).

The Letter

Personal letters should be as spontaneous and informal as the relation between writer and his correspondent permits. They should usually be dated in the upper right hand corner and should usually be punctuated with a comma after the salutation.[4]

If it is desirable to include the name and address of the person to whom the letter is written, this may be placed after the body of the letter, flush with the left hand margin and a few lines below the signature. Official letters regularly follow this form.[5]

25. Personal Letters

Formal social notes of announcement, invitation, acceptance, or regrets are expressed in the third person throughout, and carry no inside address or signature save the home address of the sender, which may be either engraved at the top

26. Formal Social Letters

of the paper or written below the body near the left hand margin. When a date is desirable it is written in the lower left hand corner—below the address, if there is one—and consists of the month and the day of the month, both written in full; or merely of the day of the week. The year is not indicated.

27. Business Letters   In the form of business letters there is considerable latitude. The best business firms are very particular about their letters and most of them have one exact form which they insist upon. The form given below is demanded by many large concerns.

[LETTERHEAD]

January 24, 19—

Mr. John P. Brownell,
256 Culver Street,
Columbus, Minn.

Dear Sir:

Thank you for your order of January 20.
We shipped the goods to you by freight today and enclose the bill of lading.
We believe you will find the shipment up to standard in both material and workmanship. We shall be glad to give you equally quick service at any time.

Yours truly,
Brown Boot and Shoe Company
(Signature of writer.)

1 encl.
CJ/M

a. The date may be centered under the letter-head if desired. In the date-line the month must always be written out, not indicated by a figure. For May 7, 1921, America writes 5/7/1921; Europe writes 7/5/1921. This would make an intolerable confusion in international correspondence.

b. If punctuation is to be omitted from the address, it is necessary, for the sake of uniformity, to avoid contractions that require periods at the ends of the lines.

c. The plural of *Dear Sir* is *Gentlemen.*

d. A business letter should be single-spaced within paragraphs and double-spaced between them.

e. If a letter is very short, it may look better double-spaced throughout. Increasing the margins also improves the appearance of a short letter.

f. A letter must be centered on the page, vertically as well as horizontally.

g. When the name of the firm is signed, it should be typewritten, and should precede the written signature of the writer, unless he wishes to assume individual responsibility for the contents.

h. It is a good modern practice to typewrite the signature of the writer also, and let him sign in ink over the typewritten line. This prevents errors due to illegible signatures.

i. To ensure accuracy, the number of enclosures should always be indicated.

j. The first initials in the lower left hand

28. Mechanical Details in Business Letters

corner are those of the writer of the letter; the second those of the stenographer.

k. To prevent confusion, the second page of a business letter should always carry in the upper left-hand corner the name or the initials of the addressee and the number of the page.

29. General Rules for a Business Letter

a. A business letter must be:

Clear:	Business cannot be conducted on guesswork.
Concise:	A busy man has no time to waste on useless words.
Complete:	Incomplete information means error or delay.
Concrete:	Abstract and general phrases blur the impression.
Convincing:	Convincingness comes from straight, simple face-to-face talk.
Courteous:	Modern business is built on courtesy and service.
Correct:	A carelessly written letter means a careless businessman.

b. Don't use *prox., inst., ult.* Write out the name of the month.

c. Don't write *July 25th.* The *th* adds nothing. Write *July 25.* For a second reference to the date one may write *the 25th.*

d. Don't use the headless forms: *Have sent . . . , Enclose herewith . . . , Beg to . . .* Courtesy and clearness demand: *We have sent . . . , I enclose . . . , We beg to . . .* , etc. The increased effort required is negligible, and more than pays for itself in the more personal impression conveyed.

e. Never use the absurd *same*, as in the expression *we have shipped same. Same* in such a connection always means either *it* or *them.* These words take no longer to write and are more accurate. *Same* in the business letter is a relic of the days when any business communication in writing tried to be clumsily legal.

f. Avoid such hackneyed and aimless phrases as: *I would suggest . . . , We beg to acknowledge your favor of . . . , Please find enclosed . . .* Say: *I suggest that . . . , We have your letter of . . . , We enclose . . .*

g. Never use the "participial glide" in the last sentence. *Hoping to serve you again we remain,* has the double weakness of employing the present participle, and a hackneyed phrase. The last sentence in a letter is the place for a clear-cut effective statement, not a dying-out phrase.

h. Finally, don't clutter the opening words of the first sentence with mechanical data concerning the receiving of letters, dates, and so on. Begin with a vigorous personal message to the reader and bring in the necessary data later. It is the first personal impression that counts. Strike out all the old mechanical phrases that have lost their vitality, and talk as you would talk face to face.

As a correspondence expert points out, no salesman would enter a business man's office with the words, "Yours of the 10th inst., received and contents noted." Nor would he bow himself out with "Hoping to sell you another order soon, I remain." Then why do it in a letter, which ought to be your personality on paper? In business just as in literary writing, stereotyped expressions and a mechanical impersonality take all the life out of what you have to say.

Punctuation

The earliest writing was unpunctuated. The reader was left to pick out sentence from sentence as best he could. Later it was discovered that separating sentences from each other by some sort of sign made reading easier. Later still, other marks were introduced within the sentence itself to make its structure and meaning clear to the reader at the first glance.

The best way to understand punctuation is to remember its origin. When we speak we make slight pauses or drop or raise the voice to mark off the smaller word groups—clauses, phrases, modifiers, series, etc.—of which a complete sentence is usually made up. So, too, the inflection of the voice suggests a question or an exclamation. The written word has no such interpreter, unless we use a set of symbols, as we do in music, to indicate the time, the pauses, and the modulations. The purpose of punctuation is to

30. What It Is

suggest the way in which the written word should be read aloud so as to make it as intelligible as possible. In a secondary sense, of course, punctuation helps to clarify, but this it does primarily by providing directions for the handling of the voice, the placing of emphasis, and the correct reproduction of the movement of the thought.

The period indicates the lowering of the voice at the end of a complete and independent thought. The question-mark signals for rising inflection; and the exclamation-mark calls for intensity. The semicolon—halfway between period and comma—indicates the relatively long pause with which we separate two virtually independent, antithetical, or balanced statements which for some logical reason we desire to include in a single sentence. The colon signals for that longer suspension which follows an introductory or anticipatory statement, or which separates two definitely appositional statements. The dash by its very appearance indicates a break in speech, a change in thought or structure. Finally, the comma warns the reader of all those shorter pauses which must be made between words and groups of words to prevent these groups from running together into an ambiguous and sometimes an unintelligible mass. And quotation-marks, though devised mainly for the eye, also warn us of that change in voice with which we usually introduce someone else's words. Punctuation in written speech, as the voice is spoken, indicates the logical relationship of the various elements of the thought.

Beside acting as a full stop, the period indicates abbreviations.

31. The Period

Note. The title *Miss* is not an abbreviation, neither are the forms 1*st,* 2*nd,* 4*th,* 23*rd,* etc.

I. Commas for inserted or introductory groups.

32. The Comma

Words or groups of words which are not essential to the mechanical completeness of the thought, and which more or less interrupt its flow, are usually set off or enclosed by commas. Such words are for the most part introductory adverbial expressions, qualifying or explanatory expressions, or other interrupting material. Commas before and after such expressions indicate that the expressions are parenthetical. A comma must both precede and follow such interpolations—unless the phrase begins or ends the sentence—for a single comma will merely break the sentence into two irrational parts and uselessly interrupt the movement.

Separate from the rest of the sentence by commas:

a. The vocative. *Come here, John.*

b. Words plainly in apposition. *Washington, the capital, is on the Potomac.*

c. The name of a county, state, or country indicating the location of a town. *We live in Hanover, New Hampshire, most of the year.*

d. An interrupting exclamation—*of course, to be sure,* etc., a transitional phrase—*now, still, thereafter,* etc., or a purely logical connective—*however, nevertheless,* etc., except when they are so closely knit into the thought movement that a break would be clumsy.

e. A separable—or *non-restrictive*—modifying clause or phrase, which may be: a relative clause; or a group of words in apposition; or a group which modifies a substantive, an adjective, an adverb, or a verb.

Such clauses or phrases are *separable* only when they may be taken bodily out of the sentence without actually changing its meaning. *Non-separable* clauses or phrases are those which are essential to the exact meaning of the sentence; they *must not be separated* from the rest of the sentence by commas.

Separable:—*This water, which is stagnant, is bad to drink.*

Non-separable:—*Water which is stagnant is bad to drink.*

Separable:—*He went directly, as he always could, to the heart of the matter.*

Non-separable:—*He went as directly as he could to the heart of the matter.*

f. Introductory expressions of time or manner, whenever the absence of a comma leads to a momentary ambiguity in the reader's mind.

Necessary:—*Soon after, dinner was announced.*

Unnecessary:—*Late in the evening dinner was announced.*

g. The salutation of a personal letter.

h. An expression introducing or interrupting a direct quotation. *"The town,"* she answered, *"is five miles away."*

II. Commas for structurally essential groups.

In everyday speech there are pauses that mark the dividing line between parallel constructions and between words in a series; pauses that break up a sentence into its component parts; pauses that indicate co-ordinate and subordinate elements in the sentence; and pauses that serve in general to prevent ambiguity. In writing, commas have to do the work of these pauses.

The insertion of commas in order to prevent ambiguity should, if possible, be avoided by re-phrasing the sentence so as to make it intelligible without such pauses.

Moreover, one must always take care to avoid, as far as possible, the putting in of *one interrupting* comma between such closely related parts of a sentence as the subject and the verb, and the verb and its object. Remember that the purpose of commas is to hold apart, for the sake of clearness, more or less independent parts of a sentence (as the comma that follows), or to inclose and segregate more or less parenthetic material (as *for the sake of clearness* in the preceding clause).

i. Words or groups of words in a parallel construction ought usually to be separated from each other by commas.

To the right of us, to the left, and in front the waves broke ominously.

Note. If the parallel constructions, however, are clauses of considerable importance and independence, semicolons or even colons may be desirable. (See the first sentence under II above.)

j. Words, phrases, or clauses in a series should be separated by commas (as in this sentence). The writing of *and* between the last two members of the series does *not*—unless there is some specially close connection between these two members—make it possible to leave out the comma. *He sold coffee, tea, and cocoa.*

The comma is, of course, not necessary if conjunctions such as *and* or *or* or *nor* are introduced between all the members of the series.

Moreover, commas are not thrust in between two, sometimes even three, adjectives when these adjectives are short familiar words which combine with the noun to give a single unified impression. *This new modish hat costs only six dollars.*

k. A dependent clause should usually be separated from a principal clause by a comma unless the sentence is short and the meaning unmistakable. The comma may be omitted from a conditional sentence if the conditional clause follows—as in this sentence. If, however, the conditional clause precedes, it is usually necessary to insert a comma to indicate the junction of the two clauses—as in this sentence.

l. Antithetical clauses connected by *but,* or *yet,* or some other disjunctive expression should usually be separated by commas. *He came early, but the car had gone.*

Where the sentence is short and closely knit, however, the comma may be omitted. *He tried but failed.*

m. A comma is used to separate the day of the month from the year—*November 25, 1921*—in order to avoid confusion between the two sets of figures. There is no comma between the month and the day of the month.

33. The Semicolon

a. In a compound sentence, independent clauses which are not joined by conjunctions should usually be separated by semicolons. If the movement of the thought is rapid and the elements closely related, however, a comma may be desirable, for a comma breaks the flow far less than the more formal semicolon or the still more formal colon.

b. To avoid confusion semicolons may be used to separate clauses or groups of words which contain commas within themselves.

Note. In ordinary writing the long sentence which demanded semicolons is going out of fashion. This does not mean that a long sentence should be inadequately punctuated with commas alone, but that sentences are being more carefully phrased and more closely knit.

34. The Colon

a. A colon may be used to draw attention to two appositional or strongly contrasted statements. *King George is king of England: Lloyd George is its ruler.*

b. A colon is useful in marking off an introductory or anticipatory statement from the matter which follows, or in introducing a formal list or statement. Hence the colon after the salutation of a business letter.

c. A colon should be used to separate a long

or formal quotation from an introductory statement.

Note. In ordinary dialogue, the comma is used to introduce a quotation.

35. The Dash a. A dash should be used after an incomplete phrase, clause, or sentence.

b. A dash is often used to indicate an abrupt break in the thought or construction of a sentence—a break too abrupt for commas, but not abrupt enough to demand the unsightly parentheses.

Note. Ordinarily do not combine a dash with a comma. The dash is complete in itself.

36. Quotation Marks a. Quotation marks are used to indicate the exact words quoted. Indirect quotations introduced by *that* are not set off by quotation marks.

b. All punctuation belonging strictly to the words quoted must be included within the quotation marks.

c. A period is not put at the end of a quotation unless the end of the quotation coincides with the end of the sentence in which it appears. A comma is the usual punctuation at the end of a quotation which is followed by further statements within the same sentence.

"I am ready," he said.

d. If the end of the quotation is also the end of the whole sentence, the period is put inside the quotation marks.

He said, "I am ready."

e. If commas are used to set off an explanatory statement which is interpolated between two passages of quotation, the commas in each case stand before the quotation marks.

"I asked you," he said, "to come with me." In this case the comma after *you* does not belong to the quotation, but serves to set off the interpolation *he said.*

Note. In other words, commas and periods when combined with quotation marks always precede the quotation marks. All other marks of punctuation fall within or without the quotation marks according as they apply to the quotation alone or to the whole sentence in which the quotation is embedded.[6]

Did he say, "I am ready"?
He said, "Are you ready?"

f. A quotation within a quotation must be indicated with single quotation marks. A quotation within a quotation within a quotation must be indicated with the usual double marks, and so on in alternation.

g. When a series of consecutive paragraphs is quoted, quotation marks precede each paragraph and follow only the last paragraph.

h. In writing dialogue it is best to begin a new paragraph whenever a new person speaks.

37. The Hyphen

a. When a word is divided and hyphenated at the end of a line it must be divided only between syllables. When in doubt write the whole word on one line.

b. Words or terms compounded of two or more words should be hyphenated except where common usage writes them as one word.

Roommate, president-elect, would-be orator.

Note. This rule may be amplified by pointing out that custom inclines toward using the hyphen where each of the two words joined keeps a distinct accent of its own, as in *timber-mill,* but drops the hyphen where the two words so far coalesce as to have but one distinctly accented syllable, as in *millwheel.*

c. The hyphen should be used in spelling out fractions, such as *two-thirds, eight-tenths,* and in compound numbers like *thirty-seven* or *four thousand and fifty-three,* where the hyphen indicates the omission of *and* from the old form *fifty and three.* In such forms unless the digit is connected by a hyphen with the tens figure we may have such ambiguous expressions as *fifty two wheeled carts,* where the *two* may be taken either with *fifty* or with *wheeled.*

Note. In typewriting care should be taken to distinguish between the hyphen and the dash by writing the dash with a space before and after. This is better practice than using two hyphens to indicate a dash.[7]

38. The Parenthesis and the Bracket a. The parenthesis ( ) is used to enclose some explanatory statement made by the writer but not grammatically connected with the sentence into which it is inserted. The dash has now largely usurped the place of the parenthesis within the sentence.

Note. In manuscripts *never* put a parenthesis around words which have been written by mistake. Cross out such words by running a line through them. The use of the parenthesis in such cases is illogical and confusing.

b. The bracket [   ] is used to enclose words inserted in the manuscript by someone else than the original writer. An editor may employ it in annotation, or a reporter when he wishes to indicate applause in a verbatim report of a speech. [*Applause*].

39. The Apostrophe

a. The apostrophe is used to indicate contraction within a word or between two words: *fo'c's'le* for *forecastle*, *can't* for *cannot*, *it's* for *it is*.

Note. Do not confuse *it's*, the contraction, with *its*, the possessive of the neuter pronoun.

b. The apostrophe is used to connect the possessive *s* with its noun.

When a word, whether singular or plural, does not already end in an *s*, the apostrophe stands between the s and the word. *The boy's parents. The children's home.* When a word, whether singular or plural, already ends in an *s*, the apostrophe stands after the *s* and a second *s* is not added. *James' room. The students' holiday.*[8] There is, however, good usage to justify the adding of another *s* in forming the possessive of proper names already ending in *s*, particularly when the name is used in the plural, as—*The Jones's car.**

Where a group of words takes the possessive, the apostrophe and the *s* follow the last word in the group. *Somebody else's hat* not *Somebody's else hat. The son-in-law's return.*

This usage sometimes leads to an amusing ambiguity as in the familiar catch: "*Moses was the son of Pharaoh's daughter, and Moses was the daughter of Pharaoh's son.*" These statements are both correct (in a figurative sense, at least), but the second can be written less ambiguously by using hyphens: "*Moses was the daughter-of-Pharaoh's son.*"

Note. The possessive pronouns *hers, ours, yours,* and *theirs* are not written with the apostrophe.

Whose is the possessive of *who,* and not *who's* or *whose'.*

c. The apostrophe is used to indicate the plurals of letters, figures, signs, and words that have no plural of their own. *Dot your i's. Three 4's. A dozen I. O. U's. Many and's make a sentence stringy.*

---

* The plural of Jones, according to most grammarians, is Joneses: *Keeping up with the Joneses.* The possessive plural is therefore Joneses': *The Joneses' maid.* This example in the original text appears to have been a slip.—ED.

Style

A writer's style is his own distinctive way of expressing his personality in vocabulary, idiom, and sentence structure. Another man's style cannot be consciously copied without plagiarism. In fact, trying to imitate another's style is much the same thing as trying to disguise one's identity behind a papier-mâché mask that looks like Bernard Shaw or G. K. Chesterton. It might be amusing for a fancy dress ball, but only a lunatic would attempt to go about that way in ordinary life.

For all that, it is well worth our while to observe and analyze the different ways in which different writers write the same language. A comparison of styles calls our attention to the infinite variety of music and effect produceable, and it also serves to remind us of the difference between an accurate expression of thought and individuality—which is style—and the ordinary careless stringing together of words that perhaps achieves intelligibility—but achieves nothing more.

The books listed below offer a wide variety of styles—most of them excellent in their own way —and illustrate also the discussions of paragraphing, sentence structure, vocabulary, and punctuation in this book. The descriptive notes mention only a few of the more distinctive qualities of the writers named.

The English Bible in the King James Version: for the majesty of its rhythm, and the dignified simplicity of its diction.

Orthodoxy or *Heretics* by G. K. Chesterton: for the clearness with which the ideas are flashed upon us by antithesis and paradox.

Youth or *The Nigger of the "Narcissus"* by Joseph Conrad: for the almost Biblical sweep of the rhythm, and the richness of the phrasing.

The Financier by Theodore Dreiser: as an illustration of excellent material embogged in a style overburdened with detail and lumbering in construction.

The Patrician or *The Forsyte Saga* by John Galsworthy: for the smooth, dignified, well-modulated, yet emotionless style.

Life's Handicap (or *Stories of Mine Own People*) by Rudyard Kipling: for the activity of its verbs—the vigor and simplicity of its whole vocabulary.

Virginibus Puerisque by Robert Louis Stevenson: for its delicate rhythm and its subtly chosen—if slightly artificial—vocabulary.

NOTE: The publisher of the 1963 edition suggests, among others, the following recently published books as illustrating some of David Lambuth's principles:

The Art of Scientific Investigation by W.I.B. Beveridge
The Powers of Poetry by Gilbert Highet
Of Stars and Men by Harlow Shapley
Cybernetics by Norbert Wiener

On Business Writing

by Walter O'Meara

In what special ways do the rules so lucidly set forth in David Lambuth's little book, "On Writing," apply to business prose?

We in business are perhaps the most prolific writers of all time. Our output of letters, reports, memoranda, and so on is staggering—and, according to our critics, mostly dreadful. It is, we are told, pompous, obscure, hackneyed, ungrammatical, and loaded with vulgarisms like "finalize" and "guesstimate."

If we must plead guilty to much of this, at least we are in distinguished company. Economists, art critics, book reviewers, psychologists, all have their favorite bromides: "Consumeristic economy," "levels of experience," "concrete pictorial sensations," "psychical apparatus." In what respect, we may ask, are such elegant clichés different from the quaint folkspeak of the business community?

Jargon is jargon, no matter where you find it; and the only place you find it is not, by any means, in business writing. But that, of course, does not absolve us of our own sins; and businessmen themselves are increasingly concerned about the generally low level of office prose. Many large organizations, indeed, have set up "writing clinics" and other programs for the improvement of so-called Business English.

The Communication Problem

As Heagan Bayles has pointed out, the cost of confusion comes high in the business world. Clarity, as well as time, is money. So the problem of communication in writing is a practical one. It is also baffling.

"Why is it," a corporation president asks, "that so many well-spoken executives become semiliterates when confronted with a blank sheet of paper?"

"Why," a sales manager wants to know, "can't my men write as clearly as they talk—in simple, natural, ordinary English?"

The head of an advertising agency fights his way through this paragraph in an account executive's report:

> The basis, constant on every account except this one, we have been using for these memorandums on sales is the comparative for the 1961 calendar year sales with the average for the past three years.

"Now why," he asks wistfully, "should anybody write a sentence like that one?"

Such questions, it has been hinted darkly, are

really for the psychologists to answer. Pompous phrases, impressive clichés, ambiguity, obscurity —all these may be no more than the unconscious defenses of insecure men fearful of committing themselves.

One thing does seem clear: bad business writing does not necessarily reflect a want of formal education. Some of the worst offenders, many executives report, are fresh out of college. It would be difficult, for that matter, to outdo the pretentious prose that is almost standard in the estimable *Harvard Business Review*. A fair sample:

> Though not basically concerned with how promotion gets its job done—not requiring absolute proof of promotion's value—management does want a logical rationale supported by dollar evaluation.

Young men in business often emulate writing that would move any city editor to throw a rewrite man downstairs, typewriter and all. They mistake it for the language of success. Later on, they learn that really successful men—the "men at the top"—usually write in clear, simple English.

In this book David Lambuth and his collaborators tell us how to write clear, simple English. Be concise. Excise every unnecessary word, sentence, paragraph. Use active verbs and concrete nouns. Shun adjectives. Write simple sentences with short Anglo-Saxon words. And so on.

The rules are plain and well-established, and

The Rules Are Plain

there are no special ones for Business English. No matter who is writing what, the accepted principles of grammar and good usage are always the same. It must be admitted, however, that businessmen have their own special ways of breaking the rules; and it may be useful to examine some of them.

Exhibit number one is the cliché, sometimes called "businessese." Every trade and profession has its stereotypes, as we have noted; but the businessman has borrowed so happily from all of them that his prose sags under the tired locutions of economics, psychology, government, sociology, sports, the space agencies, as well as those he has thought up for himself.

Be Warned and Beware! A sampling of current business clichés would include: top-level, categories, bench mark, corporate image, know-how, top-management, within the framework of, implement, spell out, budgetwise, equate with, broaden the base, effectuate, facet, update, educated guess, concretize. And there are hundreds more.

This, E. B. White warns young writers, is "the language of mutilation." Yet, there is nothing really wrong with most of these words. It is just that they are staggering from overwork and deserve a rest. Let them have it.

There are fashions in clichés. Not long ago, "historical" was a popular one. It made ordinary statements sound important: "Historically, sales have increased every year since 1958." Currently, "area" is a favorite: "Significant opinions pattern fairly well in several areas of concern to us." If you must use such commonplaces, at least keep in style; there is nothing worse than an old-fashioned cliché.

Besides clichés, various odd turns of speech, hard to classify and even harder to understand, have crept into Business English. One is "from here on in." Perhaps the extra preposition is for emphasis; but if so, wouldn't "from here on in out" be even more emphatic? And how about "from here on in out up"?

Look twice at every sentence you write—just to make sure it really makes sense.

It is easy to put together a string of simple, short, strictly Anglo-Saxon words that add up to nonsense. Simplicity alone is not enough. The difference between plain talk and claptrap, between lucidity and puerility, can indeed be very thin. Important as style may be, it is less important than what you have to say.

Simplicity Is Not Enough

So, perhaps we should take a close look at exactly what is meant by simplicity in business writing.

In their instructive provocative book, *Is Anybody Listening?*, William H. Whyte, Jr., and the editors of *Fortune* have defined true simplicity very well:

> In the meantime, let us not forswear the richness and infinite variety of our language. It is only the illusion of simplicity that this can give

us. Simplicity is an elusive, almost complex thing. It comes from discipline and organization of thought, intellectual courage, and many other attributes more hard-won than by short words and sentences. Plain talk—honest plain talk—is not the means to simplicity; it is the reward of it.

One executive makes this concrete with: "Half the memos I get are almost unreadable. And why are they almost unreadable? Because *they haven't been thought through.*"

People who aren't sure about what they want to say tend to use long Latin words, involved sentences, the passive voice, and expressions like "We will structure our planning pursuant to your thinking." Bad English can result from confusion, as well as confusion from bad English.

No Time for Cryptograms In business writing especially, it is important to arrange your thoughts and present your ideas clearly. Busy executives have no time for cryptograms. Nothing irks them so much as a confused and incoherent piece of writing. And nothing disposes them so favorably toward a subordinate as a concise, cogent one, such as:

> The client approved the entire campaign with enthusiasm and okayed the budgets for all media.

We cannot always write *that* well, of course; but no matter what you have to say, it will pay you to know how to organize your thoughts and marshal your ideas systematically.

The first step is to make an outline. Think for a while about what needs to be said. Sort out the important points and arrange them in a rough order—with *a beginning, a middle, and an end.* Then go to work with a pencil.

**Think—
Then Write**

Don't dictate your outline. Don't attempt to "write" it in your head. Put it on paper. It is extremely useful to *see* how your thoughts are shaping up. An outline is something like a chart; it has a definite visual value.

There is, of course, no all-purpose formula for writing an outline—each must be tailored to the job at hand. It may be helpful, however, to glance at the classic pattern for a particular form of writing in which clarity and decisive thinking are of the utmost importance—the standard military plan.

Stripped down to essentials, the steps are:

1. Estimate of the situation
2. Favorable factors
3. Unfavorable factors
4. Conclusions
5. Recommendations

This is a good example of an outline with a beginning, a middle, and an end. It is simple, practical, and leads to action. A writer following such an outline is likely to achieve a logical, organized presentation of his ideas and views. He may not write a brilliant plan; but he is not likely to write a bad one.

When you have worked up your rudimentary outline, you can begin to flesh it out with subheadings and sub-subheadings. Then call in your secretary—if you have one—and dictate your first draft. It may not quite write itself; but if your outline is sound, it will come easier—and make more sense.

For it is lack of an outline—a structural skeleton—that makes so much business writing flabby, formless, and hard to follow. When an executive complains that a report is "all over the place," he usually means that someone hasn't taken the trouble to outline his thoughts before putting them down on paper.

Hard Writing— Easy Reading

So now you have your rough draft—but not for long. At once, you will begin revising. You may add, cut, switch parts around, maybe throw the whole thing into the waste-paper basket and start over. You may wind up with half a dozen drafts before you are satisfied. Occasionally, of course, there won't be time for such thorough revision, and you must depend on a sound outline to see you through. But whenever you can, revise, revise, revise.

And rewrite. Even when you are content with the basic structure of your paper, you will continue to edit for clarity, conciseness, accuracy, and forceful expression. You will work over each paragraph, sentence, and word. You will sharpen, tighten up, smooth out. You will check grammar, usage, spelling, and punctuation. Perhaps you will find, to your horror, that you have written:

It is likely that everyone is conscious of the deteriorating sales situation which this client continues to suffer.

So you draw your pencil through those eighteen turgid words, and write in their place:

This client's sales are still off.

You will subject every sentence to the same rigorous test of clearness, conciseness, and aptness. And only then will you hand the result over to your secretary for final typing.

This may not be the easiest way to turn out a memorandum, plan, or presentation. But for most of us, it is the only way to turn out a good one. Hard writing, it has been truthfully said, alone makes easy reading. Even a simple letter deserves your best.

Tips from the Pros

The professionals—men and women who make their living from writing—have practical work-rules that you will find helpful in business writing. Here are a few:

First, don't push yourself too far. Four hours is about the limit of concentrated effort. After that, you are likely to begin writing involved sentences, hackneyed phrases. "When I find myself repeating a certain word—usually a long Latin one," says an author, "I know it is time to knock off and take a break."

Second, put your work on ice for a while, then come back to it with a fresh eye. You will be surprised to find how clearly repetitions, redundancies, and other writing faults stand out.

Third, keep on your desk—not in a bookcase—a good dictionary, a thesaurus (preferably in dictionary form), and this *Golden Book.* And use them!

Fourth, tabulate your main points, grouping them on the order of I, II, III; A, B, C; 1, 2, 3; a, b, c. This does not make for the smoothest kind of writing; but—especially in the case of long and complex documents—it will be greatly appreciated by the executive who must skim read.

Fifth, break up long stretches of solid writing with sub-captions.

Sixth, begin important paragraphs with a simple, declarative topic sentence that sums up what is to follow. This makes for clearer thinking as well as fast, easy reading.

Seventh, end your paper, or each main division of it, with a summary paragraph.

Summary

Businessmen talk clearly and forcefully, but much of their writing is pompous, cliché-ridden, ungrammatical, and obscure.

The first step toward better business writing is a mastery of the rules of English and good usage, as set forth in this booklet. These rules apply to so-called Business English exactly as they apply to other kinds of writing. Compliance with them will help you to write simply, clearly, and naturally.

But simplicity is not the only requirement of good writing. *What* we say is even more important than *how* we say it. We must, therefore, organize our thoughts so as to communicate them cogently, forcefully, and with the utmost economy of time and effort on the part of our readers.

To this end, it is necessary to outline our work carefully on paper, revise it rigorously, and re-write it with painstaking attention to every paragraph, sentence, and word. Topic sentences, tabulations, sub-captions; and a summary para-graph are useful devices.

Only hard writing makes easy reading—the kind of reading that saves time, effort, and hence money, in the high-pressure world of business.

Publishers' Appendix

In a world of change, the principles so engagingly set forth by David Lambuth and his collaborators have stood up remarkably well. Most of them are still a part of the best editorial practice in book publishing—even if they have been relaxed in newspapers and the mass magazines. At two points where our own practice differs sharply, pages 23 and 64, we have added footnotes on the page itself, to avoid misleading the reader even for a moment. The notes that follow, indicated by superscript numbers in the text, point to further but less clear-cut differences.

1 (p. 13) "center about": A purist would object to this locution. Strictly speaking, a center is a point; things cannot center *about* or *around* but must center *in* or *on* something.

2 (p. 22) "depends upon this reference being exact": We prefer "this reference's being exact," out of respect for H. W. Fowler's masterly attack (in *Modern English Usage*) on what he calls the "fused participle." But this is a fairly

innocuous example of what can become a monstrosity if abused.

3 (p. 36) "different to": This is frowned upon by most stylists; the approval it receives here is exceptional. Among the disapproved usages in this section, "in back of" and "he stayed home" are usually allowed today.

4 (p. 47): The author's preference for a comma after the salutation seems odd. Even in personal letters, a colon is correct; and a dash is common.

5 (p. 47): It is not our experience today that official letters "regularly" place the name and address at the foot rather than at the head, though either is correct.

6 (p. 61): Current practice in this respect puts all commas and periods inside quotes and all colons and semicolons outside, regardless of the sense.

7 (p. 62): This nicety has now almost disappeared; the use of two hyphens for a dash in typing is fairly general usage.

8. (p. 63): It seems more logical to us to add the s after the apostrophe when an extra s-sound is heard in the spoken word (*Henry James's novel, Wallis's husband*) and add the apostrophe without the s when the s-sound is not repeated in normal speech (*Dickens' characters, the twin brothers' clothes*). It is safe to follow the general rule—though there may be exceptions to it—that all proper names of one syllable ending in s take the added *'s* in the possessive, whereas names of more than one syllable take the added *'s* only when they end in the hard s sound, not the z sound (*Tacitus's play, Bemelmans' story*).